To the Reader…

Our purpose in creating this series is to provide young readers with accurate accounts of the lives of Native American men and women important in the history of their tribes. The stories are written by scholars, including American Indians.

Native Americans are as much a part of North American life today as they were one hundred years ago. Even in times past, Indians were not all the same. Not all of them lived in teepees or wore feather warbonnets. They were not all warriors. Some did fight against the white man, but many befriended him.

Whether patriot or politician, athlete or artist, Arapaho or Zuni, the story of each person in this series deserves to be told. Whether the individuals gained distinction on the battlefield or the playing field, in the courtroom or the classroom, they have enriched the heritage and history of all Americans. It is hoped that those who read their stories will realize that many different peoples, regardless of culture or color, have played a part in shaping the United States and Canada, in making both countries what they are today.

Herman J. Viola
General Editor
Author of *Exploring the West*
and other volumes on the West
and American Indians

GENERAL EDITOR
Herman J. Viola
Author of *Exploring the West* and other volumes on the West
and Native Americans

MANAGING EDITOR
Robert M. Kvasnicka
Coeditor of *The Commissioners of Indian Affairs, 1824-1977*
Coeditor of *Indian-White Relations: A Persistent Paradox*

MANUSCRIPT EDITOR
Eric Newman

PROJECT MANAGER
Joyce Spicer

PRODUCTION
Jack Reichard
Scott Melcer

Published by Steck-Vaughn 1993

Copyright © 1993 Pinnacle Press, Inc., doing business as Rivilo Books

Printed and bound in the United States.

1 2 3 4 5 6 7 8 9 0   WO   98 97 96 95 94 93

Library of Congress Cataloging-in-Publication Data

Jeffredo-Warden, Louise V.
    Ishi / text by Louise V. Jeffredo-Warden; illustrations by
Kim Fujiwara.
       p.   cm. — (American Indian stories)
    "A Rivilo book."
    Summary: When the Yahi tribe is virtually starved out of
existence by the white man's cutting off its food supply, one
survivor, Ishi, is discovered and taken to a California museum
at Berkeley where he is given a job and engages in a cultural
exchange with his new friends.
    ISBN 0-8114-6578-0   —   ISBN 0-8114-4096-6 (soft cover)
    1. Ishi, d. 1916 — Juvenile literature. 2. Yana Indians —
Biography — Juvenile literature. [1. Ishi, d. 1916. 2. Yana Indians
— Biography. 3. Indians of North America — Biography.]
I. Fujiwara, Kim, ill. II. Title. III. Series.
E99.Y23I83   1993
974'.004975 — dc20
[B]   92-8602
                                           CIP AC

ISHI

Text by Louise V. Jeffredo-Warden
Illustrations by Kim Fujiwara

A RIVILO BOOK

RSVP
RAINTREE
STECK-VAUGHN
PUBLISHERS
The Steck-Vaughn Company

Although no one will ever know his actual name, he came to be known as Ishi. *Ishi* is a word that means "man" in the Yahi Indian language. The name was given to him by his non-Indian friends. For religious reasons, Ishi never revealed his true name.

Ishi's life story is a very special one. For most of his life, he lived in a world of Yahi Indian ideas and inventions. Things such as the bow and arrow, harpoon, spear, and basket were an important part of his world. From his birth in the early 1860s until 1911, Ishi knew little of modern American society.

In 1908 Ishi became the last surviving member of his Yahi tribe. Three years later, he wandered into the world of twentieth-century California. Although he knew little about this world, it was a world in which he learned to live.

Ishi had a lasting impact on the lives of thousands of people in the new world he entered. He taught them the time-honored traditions of his people and the value of a way of life much different from their own.

The Yahi tribe belonged to a nation of California Indians called the Yana. The Yana nation was divided into four tribes. Each tribe had its own territory and its own way of speaking the Yana language.

Before white settlers arrived, the Yana lived in the foothills between the Sacramento River and Mount Lassen. Mount Lassen is located in the Cascade Mountains in northeastern California. The Yahi tribe lived in a rugged area there that was full of brush-covered canyons. Steep, rough cliffs formed the canyon walls. The Mill and Deer creeks flowed through the Yahi homeland.

The Yahi lived in villages built along creek banks and on the flat ledges of canyon walls. The men and boys fished for salmon with spears and harpoons. They hunted deer, a favorite food, with bows and arrows. Yahi women and girls also were experts at providing food for their families. They gathered berries, clover, grass seeds, and acorns.

Much of this work had to be done during spring, summer, and fall. Winter was a more leisurely time of the year. Winter was the time for making and repairing tools and baskets. It was also the time for telling boys and girls stories about what the world, animals, and people were like long ago. One story the children heard was about the sun.

The people went out to hunt, but they couldn't stay long. The sun came up at the center of the earth then, and so the sunset came too quickly. This was a problem for the people! "What shall we do about it?" they wondered.

The people got together and decided, "If the sun came up farther to the east, and not right above us, it would be all right."

The people then asked Cottontail Rabbit and Blue Squirrel to help. "We need to move the sun," the people told them. "Will you help us?"

Cottontail Rabbit said, "Yes. We will do it." The people wanted to know how. Cottontail Rabbit told them, "We will carry it on our backs."

"But where will you put it?" they asked him.

He answered, "We will put it on the mountain far off to the east."

Then Cottontail Rabbit began to carry the sun on his back. When he got tired, he gave it to Blue Squirrel. Finally, Cottontail Rabbit and Blue Squirrel carried the sun far, far away—to the place where it now comes up.

Life was not always easy for the Yahi. Sometimes— often toward the end of a long winter—they almost starved because their food supplies ran low. Still, they loved their life in the foothills. It was a place where the Yahi had lived for at least three thousand years.

Then it happened. It was an event from which the Yahi would never recover. In 1848 gold was discovered in California. To reach the gold fields, prospectors and other settlers came over a route called the Lassen Trail. The trail cut through the very heart of the Yahi homeland.

From the start, most of the people who came over the Lassen Trail feared or hated Indians. This made it difficult for the Yahi and the other Yana peoples to live in peace.

Hundreds of Yana were shot on sight or killed in village raids. Many were forced into slavery. For these reasons, the Yahi were afraid to go where they might be seen and shot or captured. Many areas where they hunted for deer, fished for salmon, or gathered grass seeds or acorns became dangerous places for them to visit. The Yahi were cut off from their fishing, hunting, and gathering grounds. They were forced to live where settlers on foot or horseback could not enter. The Yahi began to starve.

They also began to fight back, however, with every skill and resource they had. Time and time again, they raided the white settlers' cabins. The settlers were killing the Yahi, so the Yahi began to kill them, too.

White settlers kept pouring over the Lassen Trail by the thousands. By 1859 the Yahi were reduced to a life of constant raiding. They were so hungry they sometimes risked their lives for a few ears of corn or other vegetables.

It was during those violent times, probably in 1862, that Ishi was born. As a young boy, Ishi experienced many terrifying things. As he grew, conditions for his people became even worse.

In 1865 three settlers were killed by Indians at a place far south of Yahi territory. The settlers' hatred of Indians grew stronger. Many settlers joined together to form vigilante groups. These are groups of people who take the law into their own hands. The vigilantes combed the countryside killing any Indians they could find. By 1868 most of the Yana nation (once numbering two thousand Indians) had been killed. Even those Yana who worked for the settlers were not safe from the vigilantes.

Only a few Yahi remained alive by 1872. Ishi, who was then about ten years old, his mother, and thirteen or fourteen others fled still farther back into the canyons of Mill Creek. There, they cleverly hid themselves.

Their camp, hidden by an arching rim of trees, was invisible to anyone looking down into the canyon. The Yahi used the dense clumps of brush growing on the rocky slopes to further hide their homes. They crawled on their hands and knees over paths that went under and around—not through —the brush. When a branch was in the way, they silently bent it back. The sound of chopping or breaking would have given them away.

The Yahi trapped the animals that they ate. Chasing the animals would have attracted too much attention. They hid their campfire sites underneath rocks. They leapt from boulder to boulder, walked in streams, and scrambled up and down the steep cliffs on ropes of milkweed fiber. In so doing, the Yahi never left a footprint behind them. When they did walk on the ground, they covered each footprint with leaves, removing all proof of their existence.

The Yahi were eventually spotted and forced to flee. This time they went to a place along Deer Creek where bears once made their dens. Sometime after 1894, a place called Wowunupo mu tetna, or "Grizzly Bear's Hiding Place," became their new home.

It was at Wowunupo mu tetna that Ishi, his mother, his sister, and an elderly man spent their remaining years together as a group. All the others had long since died. How and why, no one will ever know. It was customary that Yahi not talk at length about the dead.

The unexpected end to their life in hiding came on November 9, 1908. Several white men came into the area to survey, or measure, the land. Two of them saw Ishi standing on a boulder beside Deer Creek. Ishi was looking for salmon to spear when he suddenly saw the two men. Ishi was terrified. He did not know what to do! He waved his spear through the air motioning for the men to go away. The startled surveyors went back to their camp.

The next morning, the surveying party continued its work. The surveyors began chopping through the brush-covered canyon. Ishi, on the lookout, watched their movements. As soon as the surveyors stumbled upon Wowunupo mu tetna, Ishi alerted the others.

In an instant, the old man and Ishi's sister ran, disappearing into the canyon. When the surveyors began to look around, they saw no one. Then they came upon Ishi's trembling mother, hidden under some blankets.

A few of the surveyors felt sorry for her because she looked as if she might die of fright. Ishi's mother had been hidden because she was old and ill. She would not have managed to escape. Her legs, badly swollen, were bandaged in buckskin. These surveyors gave her some water and tried to reassure her. However, they did not take her back to their camp to care for her. Instead, some of the surveyors took all the animal-skin blankets, tools, and food. They left nothing for Ishi's people.

19

After that morning, Ishi searched and searched for his beloved sister and the old man. He could not find them. Ishi thought that they probably drowned trying to cross Deer Creek. Ishi then returned to his mother—the only person left in his life. He carried her to another hiding place.

Within a short time, she died. Ishi was shattered. His world was destroyed. His loved ones were gone forever.

For the next three years, Ishi lived a lonely life without any human companions. Then, when he was almost fifty years old, Ishi could stand this way of life no longer. He was without hope. Ishi was so lonely that he did not care if he lived or died.

In absolute grief, he began to wander until hunger and
exhaustion finally overcame him. He collapsed in the corral
of a slaughterhouse outside the town of Oroville, about forty
miles from his home. On the morning of August 29, 1911,
Ishi, the last survivor of the Yahi world was found by a
group of butchers.

That day, the sheriff brought Ishi into Oroville. Ishi was put in jail to protect him from curious onlookers. Crowds arrived to try to get a look at this Indian whom they had read about in the newspapers.

The newspapers reported that Ishi was the last surviving member of a tribe "long believed to be extinct." It was reported that the tribe was "wiped from the face of the earth by the white man." The newspapers also stated that Ishi did not speak English or Spanish or the language of Indians living in the Oroville area.

The newspaper stories were noticed by two professors from the University of California at Berkeley. These men made their livings studying the many different ways of life of the various Indian tribes in California. The professors were Alfred Kroeber and Thomas Waterman. Professor Kroeber contacted the sheriff at Oroville. He asked the sheriff to hold Ishi until Professor Waterman could reach Oroville by train.

Once in Oroville, Professor Waterman was taken to meet Ishi. Because the professor was knowledgeable about many California Indian tribes, he knew that Ishi's hair was burned close to his head for a reason. It was a sign that one or more of his loved ones had died. He could see that Ishi's heart was heavy and that Ishi felt terribly alone. Professor Waterman soon realized that Ishi was also afraid that he would be killed.

Professor Waterman wanted to help Ishi. Thinking that Ishi might be a Yana Indian, the professor had brought along a list of Yana words. He used the words to speak with Ishi. Ishi began to feel safe with the professor when he recognized some of the words.

The professors worked in a museum at the university. It was not unusual for American Indians to stay at the museum. Professor Waterman made arrangements to take Ishi there. On September 4, 1911, Professor Waterman and Ishi left Oroville by train, arriving at the museum around midnight.

Alfred Kroeber

The next morning, Ishi met Professor Kroeber, who was instantly impressed by Ishi's gentle and observant nature. Ishi and the professor quickly became friends.

Ishi was learning the English language and soon had a special name for the professor. Ishi had trouble pronouncing the letter *f*. He pronounced it as the letter *p*. He came to call Professor Kroeber, who was in charge of the museum, the "big chiep."

Ishi also attached sounds such as *na* or *tee* to the ends of words because that was common in his language. Because of this custom, Ishi called his other newfound friend, Professor Waterman, "Waterman-tee."

At the museum, Ishi was both a student and a teacher. From his new friends, Ishi learned many things about modern American society. He learned, for instance, to shop for groceries, to ride a streetcar, and to sign his name on his monthly paycheck. He worked as a janitor at the museum.

Ishi carefully and patiently taught his new friends at the museum some of the oldest skills. An expert craftsman, Ishi showed how he experimented with different kinds of wood when he made his bows and arrows. He showed how he shot his bow and how he hunted.

Ishi was very intelligent and knowledgeable. He showed his new friends the workings of nature. He explained the role that people play within the world of nature.

On Sunday afternoons at the museum, Ishi shared his skills with the public. He demonstrated the art of stringing a bow, making a fire, and chipping out arrowheads from stone. Ishi became a celebrity. One afternoon, more than a thousand people came to see him.

One man who watched Ishi demonstrate his talents was a doctor named Saxton Pope. Dr. Pope talked Ishi into teaching him everything he knew about using the bow and arrow. During their sessions together, they communicated by combining the English and Yana languages. Ishi called Dr. Pope "Popey." They soon became close friends.

Ishi taught his white friends more than just the skills needed to shape a bow or chip out an arrowhead. Most of all, he taught them about the patience required to perform such delicate tasks.

Before he died of tuberculosis in 1916, Ishi taught many Americans about the Yahi way of life. He taught them about kindness, courage, dignity, and self-restraint. To people caught up in the hustle-bustle of the modern world, Ishi became a symbol of a way of life that had passed for most people, Indians and non-Indians alike.

Ishi was the last survivor of his Yahi world, but the lessons he taught are the kind that last forever.

HISTORY OF ISHI

1848-49	The discovery of gold at Sutter's Mill near Sacramento, California, resulted in the famous gold rush and the invasion of the Yahi homeland.
1862	Probably the year Ishi was born.
1872	Ishi and his band moved into the canyons to hide from the whites.
1894	About this time Ishi's group settled at Wowunupo mu tetna.
1908	Ishi was seen by the surveyors.
1911	Ishi was found outside Oroville and began his life in Berkeley.
1916	Ishi died of tuberculosis.